THE
BEAUTIFUL
GAME

A BOOK OF FOOTBALL INSPIRATION

RORY CALLAN

summersdale

INTRODUCTION

Football is a game for all people in all places. The game itself is the essence of simplicity – all you really need is a ball. You don't need to travel anywhere special to play either; a game can be played on a city street, a sun-scorched patch of land or in the local park.

So what is so inspirational about football? Maybe it's the fact that your age, height, economic status, what you look like or where you come from just don't matter on a football pitch. What matters in a game of football is your talent and your character, and these cannot be measured in terms of money or status. What is measured is your ability to master the ball, your courage, discipline and determination. When we play a game of football, it is one of the few times in life that we are all treated as equals. Football inspires us because it is a great leveller, and there is something liberating about that.

The great Italian referee Pierluigi Collina neatly summed up the important role that football can play in the life of young people when he said: 'Football allows children and youngsters to be together, to socialise, to learn how to live together and achieve things together.' Through football young people learn important moral lessons – the concept of fair play, unselfishness and the need to help each other out.

Football inspires us because of the artistry of the great players: a perfectly-flighted cross from David Beckham, a Wayne Rooney bicycle kick, Lionel Messi dribbling at full speed, a Cruyff turn, a gravity-defying flick from Ronaldo, a crunching tackle from Steven Gerrard or Bobby Moore calmly strolling out of defence with the ball at his feet. When played to its optimum, football is just beautiful to watch.

Football can inspire us for these and many other reasons. The quotes in this book convey the motivation and inspiration of the legends and current stars of the game, in the hope that their words provide a new appreciation of why football really is The Beautiful Game.

YOU MUST BE FIT, BE
ABLE TO SHOOT, BE ABLE
TO USE BOTH FEET... AND
HEAD THE BALL. THERE IS
NO ONE THING.

GEORGE BEST ON HOW TO BE A
GREAT FOOTBALLER

I eat football, I sleep football.
I breathe football. I'm not mad,
I'm just passionate.

THIERRY HENRY

Success is no accident. It is hard work,
perseverance, learning, studying, sacrifice
and most of all, love of what you are
doing or learning to do.

PELÉ

I believe in keeping control of the situation... and doing the right thing at the right time. This is what football is all about. You play football by passing the ball to one another, keeping possession... showing composure and showing confidence. If you do this, it spreads throughout the whole team and we all benefit from it.

BOBBY MOORE

I always think that the best coaches are the ones with imagination... a good intensity and a good work ethic in your training sessions. These three things married together make a good coach.

ALEX FERGUSON

There are always setbacks. It's been that way since my childhood. It was often very difficult. But with my will and commitment, I've always managed to turn the page.

FRANCK RIBÉRY

They [goalkeepers] have to be good with their feet. They also have to have specialised goalkeeper training... If you're a tall goalkeeper or a short goalkeeper; if you're a goalkeeper who has great spring in his legs or a goalkeeper who doesn't – you have to get your own technique based on what works for you.

BRAD FRIEDEL

If you're good enough,
the referee doesn't matter.

JOCK STEIN

When you train a massive club, or a little third division outfit, when you go out to play football in any situation, it is always about winning. Full stop.

PEP GUARDIOLA

You can be very talented as an individual but still not make it. Technical ability is not enough – you have to match it with dedication and effort in order to differentiate yourself from the rest.

LUÍS FIGO

Courage is more than being able to stand up to a buffeting on the field of play. Courage is the ability to get up when things are getting you down. Never to know defeat, let alone accept it... Courage is skill, plus dedication, plus fitness, plus honesty, plus fearlessness. Courage is a word that should hang above your bed if you want to be a professional footballer.

BILL SHANKLY

WINNING ISN'T
EVERYTHING,

BUT WANTING TO WIN IS.

I HAD ONE THING IN MIND: GET OUT AND PLAY FOOTBALL. FOR THAT I HAD AN INNER RAGE TO SUCCEED.

ZINEDINE ZIDANE ON HIS
SPORTING YOUTH

You can't just go through a game and be
bullied. You have got to put your foot
in... you have to be up for the fight.

JACK WILSHERE

If you don't have to drag yourself off the
field exhausted after 90 minutes, you
can't claim to have done your best.

BILL NICHOLSON

In Brazil, a ball will make 200 children happy. One ball is all you need. That's what's made football so popular. Other sports find it difficult in Brazil because they are fairly expensive. All that space and, of course, the lovely weather in Brazil are other reasons for the success. Taken together, you are left with a culture that is totally geared to football. Every Brazilian is born with football in his blood.

LUIZ FELIPE SCOLARI

Talent alone isn't enough...
The players who get the best out of
themselves are those who dedicate
themselves to the job.

BRIAN ROBSON

I love football and come from a
football family... I always watched
football on the TV. I had a big interest in
it. Every chance I got to get the ball
out that's what I did.

STEVEN GERRARD

Goalkeepers need an element of insanity. Who else would stand there and allow people to shoot balls at his face or abdomen, and still think it's great? You throw yourself at the feet of the other team's strikers, you give it your all, and of course somewhere in your subconscious you know that there are healthier things to do.

OLIVER KAHN

RESULTS DIDN'T REALLY MATTER TO ME... I JUST WANTED TO ENTERTAIN PEOPLE AND ENJOY IT... THAT'S WHAT [FOOTBALL] WAS ALL ABOUT TO ME.

LEN SHACKLETON

You play football with your head...
If you don't use your head, using your
feet won't be sufficient.

JOHAN CRUYFF

I was always of the mind I would
be the one creating the problems; that
my marker would have to come
up with the solution.

IAN RUSH

My goal has always been to become a player who was as complete as possible. I believe I have achieved that, I know what I can do and I am ready to sacrifice to succeed. You do not win because you are number one, but because the team is number one.

ZLATAN IBRAHIMOVIĆ

FOOTBALL IS ABOUT BEING BRAVE –
IF YOU DO NOTHING,
AND SAY NOTHING,

THEN YOU'LL BE
NOTHING.

WHAT DID BECKHAM
DO TO BECOME A GREAT
FREE-KICK GUY? HE
GOT OBSESSED.

DANIEL COYLE

I have sacrificed so much to be where
I am and fought so hard for it... I can't
bear the idea of not trying to make the
most of every single second.

LUIS SUÁREZ

There was no easy way to get there...
It was extra runs, extra hours practising
shooting and finishing, that became
ingrained in me.

FRANK LAMPARD

At the end of the day the game is about good players. It's about getting the best out of them – putting them in the right positions, understanding the game... You don't need PowerPoint.

HARRY REDKNAPP

Work[ing] from insecurity is always good for the athletes. The one who believes that he is very good, that [he] will surely win, is condemned to failure.

VICENTE DEL BOSQUE

I didn't have the flair or natural ability of others but I was a hard worker, sticking in the hours.

GARY NEVILLE

When I was 14, I grew and started gaining muscles. So I started doing sit-ups, abs work, press-ups, strengthening my core. I'd do 100–150 reps each day... I used to wake up and start with sit-ups and abs straight away. I'd take a shower, go to school, train [for football] then go home and stretch.

ROMELU LUKAKU

I am a person who
likes to compete, who
likes to win and who
hates to lose.

CRISTIANO RONALDO

What keeps me going is my love
for the game, for doing the job I
do and for football.

ARSÈNE WENGER

I just like playing with the ball. I always
have. I play on the street even now.
When we're on vacation – it doesn't
matter where – I will go and
look for a game.

NEYMAR

A football education on the street is a great start. It's had a huge influence on my career because it makes you strong, especially when playing against older guys, and teaches you the spirit that's necessary to become a footballer and be a winner.

SERGIO AGÜERO

THERE MAY BE PEOPLE
THAT HAVE MORE
TALENT THAN YOU,
BUT THERE'S NO EXCUSE

FOR ANYONE TO
WORK HARDER
THAN YOU DO.

THE BETTER YOUR BODY IS PREPARED, THE BETTER YOU CAN DO YOUR WORK.

DENNIS BERGKAMP

I am proud because all my life I did everything for football. I spend all my whole life to improve my body, to improve my performance. I won the World Cup [at] 32 years old.

FABIO CANNAVARO

Injury [a broken leg] only made me stronger. I had done a lot of gym work in the five and a half months that I was out. It didn't affect me in a negative way, it actually had a positive effect on me mentally because I knew I had to fight in order to come back and play football.

HENRIK LARSSON

People talk about sacrificing a lot, but how many actually do? I can assure you I did... I trained every year on Christmas Day and people couldn't believe it. Even in my non-league days... On Christmas morning I got changed to train and my wife said, 'Where are you going?' I said, 'Down the park.'

STUART PEARCE

You can really achieve everything in life,
even the unthinkable, as long as you're
willing to work on yourself a little bit.

OLIVER KAHN

Every professional footballer should seek
to play at least one game at Celtic Park.
I have never felt anything like it.

PAOLO MALDINI

Although football is a sport, it represents more. It is a way for youth to develop themselves and a vehicle of communication for all people. The World Cup, for example, is a way that people from many different backgrounds can come together not only for the purpose of winning a cup, but more importantly to learn about each other through communication on and off the playing field.

EUSÉBIO

AS A GOALSCORER, YOU
ALWAYS REMEMBER ALL
YOUR GOALS. AS SOON
AS SOMEONE MENTIONS
A CERTAIN GAME TO
YOU IN WHICH YOU
SCORED YOU CAN SEE
THE GOAL IMMEDIATELY
IN YOUR MIND.

WAYNE ROONEY

My football training began watching
the Merseyside amateur leagues. I was
mesmerised by the togetherness, the
banter, the aggression...

JAMIE CARRAGHER

What kind of a goalkeeper is the
one who is not tormented by the goal he
has allowed? He must be tormented! And
if he is calm, that means the end. No
matter what he had in the past,
he has no future.

LEV YASHIN,
LEGENDARY RUSSIAN GOALKEEPER

If there's one characteristic all
great players have it's precisely
this – they all have that gene,
that competitiveness, the ability
to overcome obstacles, to fight, a
willingness to sacrifice... All players
that have achieved those things have
that: the big ones, the small ones,
the good-looking ones, the ugly ones,
the nice ones, the not-so-nice ones...
they all have that will to succeed.

ANDRÉS INIESTA

TRAINING IS: STAMINA, SPEED, STRENGTH, SKILL AND SPIRIT;

BUT THE GREATEST OF THESE
IS SPIRIT.

FAIL TO PREPARE,
PREPARE TO FAIL.

ROY KEANE

Before the great club colours were
chosen and the monumental stadiums
were raised, people just played anywhere.
They still do.

DAVID GOLDBLATT

To be the ultimate team, you must use
your body and your mind. Draw upon
the resources of your teammates. Choose
your steps wisely and you will win.
Remember, only teams succeed.

JOSÉ MOURINHO

I believe that in life, you have to be ambitious, above all other things...
My personal goal is to continue learning and surpassing myself with each day. I'm convinced that this is the mentality that will bring success. Each morning, I wake up with a desire to win more titles and to continue growing as a person.

SERGIO RAMOS

Talent is essential but is not the only
thing. If you are reliable and work hard,
you will spend many years at the top.
You can get to the top with talent but
you will have to add things to it, like a
desire to improve and a capacity
to work hard.

RAFAEL BENÍTEZ

Self-improvement is key; never getting
complacent. You should always be
prepared to listen to advice from
teammates... Learn the game from every
player you come across. Study the game.

DANIEL STURRIDGE

I am not a perfectionist, but I like to feel that things are done well. More important than that, I feel an endless need to learn, to improve, to evolve... It is my conviction that there are no limits to learning, and that it can never stop, no matter what our age.

CRISTIANO RONALDO

Who doesn't give it all,
gives nothing.

HELENIO HERRERA, INVENTOR
OF THE CATENACCIO SYSTEM WITH
INTER MILAN IN THE 1960s

Football is like a religion to me.
I worship the ball, and I treat it like a
god. Too many players think of a football
as something to kick. They should be
taught to caress it and to treat it
like a precious gem.

PELÉ

No one gets an iron-clad guarantee
of success. Certainly, factors like
opportunity, luck and timing are
important. But the backbone of success
is usually found in old-fashioned, basic
concepts like hard work, determination,
good planning and perseverance.

MIA HAMM

Every one of our players respects every one of their players and their team as a whole. But once we cross that white line most of the respect will be out the window and we will be fighting to win the game.

DAVID BECKHAM

NOBODY WHO EVER
GAVE THEIR BEST

REGRETTED IT.

THE BEST PLACE TO DEFEND IS IN THE OPPOSITION PENALTY BOX.

JOCK STEIN

Even when we lost and I walked off the pitch in tears... I was full of pride.

MICK MCCARTHY ON PLAYING IN
THE WORLD CUP IN ROME

It's a beautiful game, the best thing there is... Football is a game that is full of excitement and joy and players should not feel stress.

DIEGO MARADONA

It's always good to communicate...
but it has to be in a positive
way – you can't just annoy your
teammates by saying negative
things. If you concede a goal,
afterwards it's easy to pick out who
made the mistake. But you have to
avoid that by telling them before –
that's the real secret.

PER MERTESACKER

I would say as a youngster, work really hard and try to develop your technique... Try and get some good coaching that will give you the basics and then work hard and build up your game from there.

PETER SHILTON

There is nothing wrong with trying to win, so long as you don't set the prize above the game. There is no dishonour in defeat, so long as you play to the limit of your strength and skill.

MATT BUSBY

From when I started to play with
a ball I wanted to win everything...
motivation is something that if
you don't have it inside then
you can't provide it.

DIEGO SIMEONE

PRACTICE DOESN'T MAKE PERFECT, PERFECT PRACTICE MAKES PERFECT.

FRANZ BECKENBAUER

If you are willing to make sacrifices and to do everything that will make the collective perform better, then you have even more possibilities of winning.

FRANK RIJKAARD

At every opportunity I wanted to be kicking a ball around... every waking hour with the ball at my feet.

ALAN SHEARER

I'm a great believer in installing self-belief, especially when you are working with young players, and to a certain extent senior players too...

ERIC HARRISON, COACH WHO WAS RESPONSIBLE FOR DEVELOPING THE TALENT OF DAVID BECKHAM, RYAN GIGGS, PAUL SCHOLES, NICKY BUTT, AND PHIL AND GARY NEVILLE

THE DIFFERENCE BETWEEN
THE IMPOSSIBLE AND
THE POSSIBLE

LIES IN A PERSON'S DETERMINATION.

CUPS ARE NOT WON BY
INDIVIDUALS, BUT BY
MEN IN A TEAM WHO PUT
THEIR CLUB BEFORE THEIR
PERSONAL PRESTIGE.

JOCK STEIN

As a trainer you have to do things... You won't be a better coach by talking a lot about football or thinking about it. You have to find out by doing.

MARCO VAN BASTEN

Ian Wright was almost unique... He was not interested at all in salary or bonuses, just 'Where do I sign?'

DAVID DEIN

Whatever happens, there are always
things you could have done better.
You score two goals and you usually
feel you could have scored a third.
That's perfectionism.

ERIC CANTONA

I do a lot of individual training, for the upper-body, for speed and for finishing. I also practise free-kicks.

MESUT ÖZIL

When I was younger I worked on building power and strength in my legs to boost explosive acceleration off the mark... If you want to be quick off the mark, this is something I would focus on because acceleration can make all the difference on the pitch.

ALEX OXLADE-CHAMBERLAIN

I never react when opposition
players try and get in my head. If
you respond by saying something,
that means they're getting to you...
I get the better of them by letting
my football do the talking.

GARETH BALE

I love football
because it's the greatest
game ever and you can talk
about football forever and
it'll never run dry.

PETER SCHMEICHEL

You need passion and to spend
endless hours at developing yourself
as a coach. You also have to have
faith in your ability.

RAFAEL BENÍTEZ

From here each practice, each game, each
minute of your social life must centre on
the aim of being champions. First-teamer
will not be a correct word. I need all
of you. You need each other.
We are a TEAM.

JOSÉ MOURINHO IN A LETTER SENT
TO CHELSEA PLAYERS WHEN HE TOOK OVER
IN 2006

I visualise the game and all the potential situations beforehand, I visualise the opponent, I project myself scoring... I study the goalkeeper's strength and most importantly weaknesses.

DIDIER DROGBA

JUST KEEP GOING.
EVERYBODY GETS BETTER

IF THEY KEEP
AT IT.

EVERY GAME IS AN
OPPORTUNITY TO
CREATE MEMORIES
WHICH, WITH THE
PASSING OF THE YEARS,
WILL BE A TREASURE
TO YOU.

IAN RUSH

You never, ever lose the thrill of watching
your own shot go past the goalkeeper.

BRIAN CLOUGH

From being a little boy from the
East End, you would never think you
would get a chance to represent your
country. I am proud, privileged and
overwhelmed by how many times I
have played for England.

ASHLEY COLE

The manager always tells us to
make sure we celebrate if we score
a goal... It's important that the
fans share our joy.

PAUL SCHOLES

There is no disgrace in wanting to win,
but it has to be done the right way,
within the spirit of football.

ARSÈNE WENGER

To become a great finisher you have to
work at it – a lot. You need to practise,
practise, practise and practise until
your legs are swollen.

FREDERICO CHAVES GUEDES AKA FRED

I have the ability to isolate myself from everything that goes on around me because my motivation has always come from inside. In football you cannot afford to get overwhelmed by euphoria or sadness.

FRANK RIJKAARD

FOOTBALL GIVES A SUFFERING PEOPLE JOY.

GEORGE WEAH

In Brazil every kid starts playing
street football very early. It's in our
blood. In Rio, I also played in the
beach soccer league, barefoot.

RONALDO

When you sign a contract to play
football professionally, part of that
agreement should be an undertaking to
be a positive role model.

BRAD FRIEDEL

If you want to play a
high-energy game you obviously
need to be super fit. There's no
substitute for playing football, but
there are other things you can do
to supplement your fitness.

JACK RODWELL

PERSISTENCE CAN
CHANGE FAILURE INTO

EXTRAORDINARY ACHIEVEMENT.

FAILURE HAPPENS ALL THE
TIME. IT HAPPENS EVERY
DAY IN PRACTICE. WHAT
MAKES YOU BETTER IS
HOW YOU REACT TO IT.

MIA HAMM

Football allows children and
youngsters to be together, to socialise,
to learn how to live together.

PIERLUIGI COLLINA

Ultimately we're all big kids, we love
playing football. Regardless of what level
you play at, we all love the game.

OWEN COYLE

Since I was a child I watched tapes of Baggio, Zico and Maradona, and then I tried to replicate them just playing on my own against the wall... you have to cultivate that talent.

ANDREA PIRLO

The first thing is to roll your
sleeves up and chase harder than the
bloke in the other shirt... You've gotta
be able to fight and then you can
overcome anything.

IAN HOLLOWAY

You've got to be reluctant to be pushed
down, you keep going; it doesn't matter
what circumstances prevail... You
persevere and refuse to give in.

BOB PAISLEY

I want the ball all the time; I have to learn to be more patient. I get too excited, too nervous. I finish some games absolutely dead and my teammates tell me to calm down. But then football is my life. My girlfriend says 95 per cent... Everything is related to football.

CESC FÀBREGAS

Every disadvantage has
got its advantage.

JOHAN CRUYFF

Football is my passion. If I want to
take my mind off things, all you have
to do is give me a ball.

FRANCK RIBÉRY

The vision of a champion is someone
who is bent over, drenched in sweat, at
the point of exhaustion, when no
one else is watching.

ANSON DORRANCE,
AMERICAN SOCCER COACH

Every game I go into I think I'm
going to win and score... I'm always
100 per cent confident I'll win...
People might say that sounds big-
headed, and you don't always win of
course, but I think I'm positive and
take that into everything I do.

WAYNE ROONEY

IT'S NOT THE WILL TO WIN
THAT MATTERS –
EVERYONE HAS THAT.

IT'S THE WILL
TO PREPARE TO WIN
THAT MATTERS.

ALL KIDS WANT TO BE
FOOTBALLERS... TO
MAKE IT YOU NEED TO
WORK HARD AND MAKE
A LOT OF SACRIFICES.

LIONEL MESSI

Make an effort and sacrifice
from day one without needing anyone
to motivate you. Do extra training
when nobody is looking.

PATRICK VIEIRA

We [Manchester United] never give up,
the time to give up is when you're dead.

ALEX FERGUSON

Youth coaching is 10 per cent about kicks up the backsides and 90 per cent about arms round the shoulders. You have to let boys use their imaginations and relax. You can't play good football if you're tense – but you can be relaxed and hard-working.

ERIC HARRISON

I suffered for my art... picking up injuries all the time from diving on the pavement to stop shots.

PEPE REINA

Anyone can play [football], whether you are poor or rich. All you need is space and a ball. One's physical build is not that important... You don't have to be big and strong. You must only have a desire to play.

EUSÉBIO

Each session my dad or mum took me to Bellefield [for training]... They would then wait to bring me back... Parents have to be as keen as their kids, making sure they turn up on time, and with the right kit.

WAYNE ROONEY ON THE IMPORTANCE OF PARENTAL GUIDANCE DURING HIS EARLY YEARS WITH THE EVERTON YOUTH ACADEMY.

I DON'T BELIEVE SKILL WAS, OR EVER WILL BE, THE RESULT OF COACHES. IT IS A RESULT OF A LOVE AFFAIR BETWEEN THE CHILD AND THE BALL.

MANFRED SCHELLSCHEIDT

Having a difficult injury early on in my
career... I learned the meaning of the
expression, 'Better to be safe than sorry.'

JOLEON LESCOTT

I sometimes say to a footballer's agent:
'The difference between you and me is
that if there were no more money in
football tomorrow, I'd still be here,
but not you.'

ARSÈNE WENGER

Football is one of the world's
best means of communication. It is
impartial, apolitical and universal.
Football unites people around
the world every day.

FRANZ BECKENBAUER

IF IT IS IMPORTANT TO YOU,
YOU'LL FIND A WAY.

IF IT IS NOT, YOU'LL FIND
AN EXCUSE.

ENJOY WHAT YOU ARE
DOING, WHATEVER YOU
CHOOSE TO DO IN LIFE –
SPORT, ART, MUSIC – MAKE
SURE YOU ARE DOING
SOMETHING YOU ENJOY.

PETR ČECH

Football is about so much more than power and size. When I was a kid and I was smaller than everyone else... but once everyone grows up it comes down to talent.

LUKA MODRIĆ

Having excellent fitness levels is vitally important. You've got to make sure you work hard during the week so that you're fully prepared for the game at the weekend.

ASHLEY YOUNG

I am competitive and I feel bad when we lose... I just retreat into myself and go over the game in my head: the things that went wrong, what I did wrong, why we didn't win.

LIONEL MESSI

My biggest motivation is to improve
my ability and all-round game every day
to become the best I can possibly be
without looking back and regretting
that I hadn't done more.

JOE HART

A lot of football success is in the mind.
You must believe you are the best and
then make sure that you are.

BILL SHANKLY

The secret is never to sit back and relax. No team can keep achieving good results unless every effort is made to set your sights high... And when that game is over, that's it – whatever the result, it is behind us and we look to the next one.

BOB PAISLEY

I would rather play
with ten men than wait
for a player who is late
for the bus.

JOSÉ MOURINHO

First and foremost, it's all about collective effort... The most important thing is to have a spirit of team unity and a winning mentality.

DIDIER DESCHAMPS

Football today... thrives on aggressive defence... It means disrupting them; getting close to them, putting them under pressure and giving them no time – being a nuisance.

PHILIPP LAHM

It's a 90-minute game for sure. In fact I used to train for a 190-minute game so that when the whistle blew at the end of the match I could have played another 90 minutes.

BILL SHANKLY

THE HARDER YOU WORK,

THE HARDER IT IS
TO GIVE UP.

IT'S BETTER TO FAIL WITH YOUR OWN VISION THAN WITH ANOTHER MAN'S VISION.

JOHAN CRUYFF

When I became a footballer, I could
run hard for 90 minutes... school gave
me the strength and stamina.

BRIAN ROBSON

It's not possible to please everyone and
there is no point in trying to be what
other people think you should be.

PEP GUARDIOLA

Football is the thing I love the most in this world, and I'm happy every time I wake up, pick up my bag and walk onto the grass of the training ground. More than a privilege, it is a luxury.

XAVI

You have to be patient, you have to listen and you have to practise, and if you do those things, you've got a chance.

BOBBY CHARLTON

If I thought that my left foot needed working on... Left foot, right foot, left, right, left, right, hundreds of times.

GARY NEVILLE

I'm always trying to improve myself,
never settling for playing just
well. Constantly, every season, I'm
questioning the sports scientists and
coaches so I can get better.

RYAN GIGGS

HE WHO PLAYS FOR HIMSELF PLAYS FOR THE OPPOSITION.

HELENIO HERRERA

If we have to deprive a player of the right to make mistakes, then we'd best just hang up everything and go home.

GIOVANNI TRAPATTONI

Someone once said to me when I was a kid: 'If you're asked to do ten sprints, by all means do eleven but never do nine because you're only cheating yourself.'

ALAN SHEARER

There are only three million people in Uruguay but there is such hunger for glory... I played in the streets with my friends, barefooted. That was the way we lived.

LUIS SUÁREZ

JUST STICK WITH IT.
WHAT SEEMS SO HARD NOW

WILL ONE DAY BE YOUR
WARM-UP.

THE GREAT THING IS THAT
SOCIETY NEEDS FOOTBALL.
IF THINGS ARE BAD, THE
ONE THING THAT KEPT
WORKING PEOPLE GOING
WAS FOOTBALL.

BOBBY CHARLTON

The natural talent was there,
but I never stopped training.

KELLY SMITH

In football there is no escaping the need
to run, make contact, challenge... get
knocked over and get back up.

BOBBY ROBSON

I'm trying to improve every single area of my game. Even when I'm injured, I'm working on my upper body strength. I'm always thinking about improving.

DANIEL STURRIDGE

You have to be positive in life...
To make people smile once every day
brings a smile to my face. That's
how I've lived my life.

BRUCE GROBBELAAR

At the age of 18, I started training
with track and field coaches on the side
two times extra per week and it helped
me to get a lot faster.

JÜRGEN KLINSMANN

As a father of four, I know how important it is to get kids to eat the right things, to drink the right things, to stay healthy, to stay fit, to get out there and get off their Xbox and into a park where they are kicking a football or running around.

DAVID BECKHAM

Football! It's the most important thing of all the small things in life.

CARLO ANCELOTTI

Everything else and everyone
else's opinion doesn't really matter –
that is the best thing you can learn as a
young player. You just have to go
out there and do your best.

JOE COLE

I've never given up. And with this
attitude, you always get somewhere in
the end. Even now, at the age of 30,
I still want to win every game.

FRANCK RIBÉRY

Defeats will come, and when
they do accept them as quietly
and philosophically as I hope
you do your victories.

DUNCAN EDWARDS

THE TROUBLE WITH NOT
HAVING A GOAL IS THAT YOU CAN
SPEND YOUR LIFE

RUNNING UP AND DOWN THE FIELD AND **NEVER SCORE.**

KEEP IN MIND THAT
FOOTBALL IS A GAME:
HAVE FUN. WIN, SHARE
AND PASS ON THE
JOY OF DOING IT
TOGETHER.

LOUIS SAHA

I was always a little behind the others...
But you have to believe that if you're
good enough, then eventually
you'll squeeze in.

PAUL SCHOLES ON STAYING PATIENT AND
DETERMINED WHILE WAITING TO BREAK
INTO MANCHESTER UNITED'S FIRST TEAM

Work hard every day. Because when
you have some limitations, you need to
improve your character, your quality.

FABIO CANNAVARO

I like players to know and to feel that I'm going to defend them like a father would his children... If I didn't, then I wouldn't be able to convey that sense of protection.

LUIZ FELIPE SCOLARI

If you are fearful you don't make
the next steps. If you are frightened to
lose, you don't do enough of what
it takes to win a game.

BRENDAN RODGERS

Everyone doubts. We all need to doubt.
If you don't doubt you can't prepare
yourself for what will happen... You have
to conquer your doubts.

ERIC CANTONA

I made sacrifices by leaving
Argentina, leaving my family to start
a new life. I changed my friends, my
people. Everything. But everything
I did, I did for football, to
achieve my dream.

LIONEL MESSI

IF YOU ONLY EVER
GIVE 90 PER CENT IN
TRAINING THEN YOU
WILL ONLY EVER GIVE
90 PER CENT WHEN
IT MATTERS.

MICHAEL OWEN

I was always thinking about being involved
in football... I always think it is important
to watch and learn and try to get better
and improve. I am no different now.

DAVID MOYES

I was good but I also used to practise
a lot... When I was younger I used to
go to the park and practise with me dad
– practise me skills, me shooting
and me free kicks.

PAUL GASCOIGNE AKA GAZZA

I went from school to football practice and from football practice to school, that was it for me. My friends went out to party, and I had to say at home because the next day I had to train... But it's OK, because now I can say it was all worth it.

SERGIO RAMOS

SUCCESSFUL PLAYERS
NEVER WORRY ABOUT

WHAT OTHERS
ARE DOING.

THERE'S NOTHING WORSE
THAN NOT MAKING THE
MOST OF YOUR ABILITIES.
BE PROUD TO SAY YOU
WORK HARD.

ALEX FERGUSON

God makes me play well... I feel I would
be betraying Him if I didn't.

DIEGO MARADONA

I have demonstrated a resilience and I
know that is important because your
players and staff look to you for direction
and they need to see... that you are in
control. Even if you aren't always feeling
in total control as a leader you certainly
need to look like you are!

ALLY MCCOIST

When I was a kid, my friends would call me to go out with them, but I would stay home because I had practice the next day. I like going out, but you have to know when you can and when you can't... My friends would go out and I'd stay home... I was dedicated to football.

LIONEL MESSI

It was a difficult time for me, but I learnt from it. I think I've become a better player for it. If you're not playing, you watch other players to see what you could be doing to improve your game.

GARETH BALE ON THE VALUABLE LESSONS LEARNED AFTER HE SUFFERED A CAREER-THREATENING INJURY IN 2007

If you do a 5,000-metre run, you're a lot slower by yourself than running in a group because you get pulled along during the tough parts... You only develop if you have good players next to you and when every game is a challenge.

MICHAEL BALLACK

As a midfielder you have to have vision. If you see an opening that might create an opportunity, you have to believe in yourself and go for it; a 40-yard pass or an eye-of-the-needle ball.

AARON RAMSEY

Behind every kick of
the ball there has to
be a thought.

DENNIS BERGKAMP

What matters above all is that the game should be played in the right spirit, with the utmost resource of skill and courage... the result accepted without bitterness or conceit.

MATT BUSBY

Every football player when they are young, wants to touch the ball and score goals; to be the hero. I always played striker when I was younger.

YAYA TOURÉ

On a usual day I will start with the keepers in the gym... After that we either go outside and join the rest of the team or stay and work on specific injury prevention exercises... On an average day I will arrive at 9 a.m. and be here until around 3 p.m.

PETR ČECH ON THE EXTENT OF
HIS PHYSICAL TRAINING

UNSUCCESSFUL PLAYERS
JUST HATE, BLAME AND COMPLAIN.

SUCCESSFUL PLAYERS
BUILD EACH OTHER UP. THEY
MOTIVATE, INSPIRE
AND PUSH EACH OTHER.

FOOTBALL IS A
SIMPLE GAME BASED
ON THE GIVING AND
TAKING OF PASSES,
OF CONTROLLING THE
BALL AND OF MAKING
YOURSELF AVAILABLE TO
RECEIVE A PASS.

BILL SHANKLY

If you want to be successful you have
to have a good worth ethic. You have to
work for your teammates.

BRIAN ROBSON

Sometimes you win matches in
unusual places – often before you
put a foot on the field.

BRIAN CLOUGH

A manager must buy cheap and sell dear. If another manager rings to ask me about a player I'll say, 'He's great, super lad, goes to church twice a day. Good in the air, two lovely feet, make a great son-in-law.' You never tell them he couldn't trap a bag of cement.

TOMMY DOCHERTY

Football is a team game so
that is the main thing. I work hard
for the team, and the good of the
group is what's important.

FERNANDO TORRES

A good routine teaches you... about
yourself and it instils some hardcore
discipline which is essential in football.

DIETMAR HAMANN

For young boys in mining villages...
To master football was to escape
the material world, the uncertainties,
the frustration, the pain.

EAMON DUNPHY

I'M NEVER GOING TO
REST ON MY LAURELS,
AND I'M NEVER GOING
TO GET COMPLACENT
OR COMFORTABLE... I'VE
GOT TO KEEP PUSHING
MYSELF, BECAUSE
NOBODY ELSE WILL.

DANIEL STURRIDGE

No matter what size you are
you can get into a position where
you can receive the ball.

JOHN GILES

You can be disappointed for two
minutes then you must prepare.

GÉRARD HOULLIER ON HIS MENTAL GAME

We [England] know that all the talking in the world... doesn't really matter because when we cross that white line... and the referee blows his whistle, in that 95 or 96 minutes when we'll actually be playing, that's when it will all count.

ROY HODGSON

REMEMBER, IF YOU ARE
NOT PLAYING YOUR
HEART OUT,

SOMEONE ELSE IS.
AND WHEN YOU MEET THEM,
THEY WILL WIN.

I LIKE BEING FIRST,
BECAUSE SECOND IS NO
GOOD. BEING SECOND IS
A FAILURE. SHOWS ARE
FOR THE CINEMA, FOR THE
THEATRE... FOOTBALL IS
PLAYED TO WIN.

CARLOS BILARDO

If the team buys into this ethos
and you all believe in it, there's harmony
between all the players and the
team becomes stronger.

FRANCO BARESI

Physically I train very hard every day.
After training, I stay every day to work
alone in the gym.

NEMANJA MATIĆ

I don't need a boring book by Freud
to show me how to read people.
I've been doing it since day one
in management. I can tell, from
the moment I see someone in the
dressing room, whether he's off
colour, had a row with his missus,
kicked the cat or just doesn't fancy
it that particular day.

BRIAN CLOUGH

I decided I didn't want to do anything that works against my body. The day after drinking you are not the same person. You are not thinking the same, you can't reach the same level.

ROBERTO MARTÍNEZ

To win is not the most important thing, football is an art, it is a way of showing creativity. You have to enjoy doing the art and not think 'will I win?'

SÓCRATES

I want to give good players the opportunity to be the best they can be. I want to make them successful. If that is too much hard work for them, if they have not got the mental strength, they are not going to come on this journey.

MARK HUGHES

It's not about the name
on the back of the jersey,
it's about the badge
on the front.

DAVID BECKHAM

Attitude is just as important as ability...
The fellas who played in the World Cup
final were not just world-class players –
they were professional people
with a great attitude.

GEOFF HURST

I think you need a great deal of courage,
physical and moral courage to do all the
things that contribute to scoring a goal.
It's not a matter of just getting into
position... you've got to have the
guts to make it happen.

JIMMY GREAVES

I used to love getting the ball and playing with it at night time on the street, under a lamppost... I always walked a lot... and got used to doing exercises from a young age.

STANLEY MATTHEWS

SOMETIMES YOU HAVE TO CHOOSE
BETWEEN THE PAIN
OF DISCIPLINE

OR THE PAIN OF REGRET.

THERE ARE TOO MANY
DEFENSIVE TEAMS
AROUND, WITH PLAYERS
PASSING THE BALL
SIDEWAYS INSTEAD OF
GOING FOR IT. I LIKE MY
PLAYERS TO HAVE FUN
AND ATTACK.

ZICO

You don't struggle for inspiration [at] this great football club, the single biggest source for me is when I arrive each match day and see the Hillsborough memorial... You [the families of the 96 victims] all stood for 25 years together [and] the love for the people you lost inspires me every day as manager... You will never walk alone.

BRENDAN RODGERS, FROM HIS SPEECH AT THE 25TH ANNIVERSARY OF THE HILLSBOROUGH DISASTER ON 15 APRIL 2014

When I was growing up I always had to play against my brother's friends who were five or six years older... this definitely helped me to improve. I had to prove myself as a small but strong dribbler. It was good experience for me.

MESUT ÖZIL

I don't believe there is such a thing as a 'born' soccer player. Perhaps you are born with certain skills and talents, but quite frankly it seems impossible to me that one is actually born to be an ace soccer player.

PELÉ

Everything that looks so effortless in public is the product of hard work from Monday to Friday. The intensity on the training ground... is a marker.

KARL-HEINZ RUMMENIGGE

There is no room for criticism on the training field. For a player – and for any human being – there is nothing better than hearing 'well done'.

ALEX FERGUSON

I always like to picture the game the night before: I'll ask the kit man what kit we're wearing, so I can visualise it... It helps to train your mind to situations that might happen the following day.

WAYNE ROONEY

PREPARING YOUR TACTICAL FORMATION IS ESSENTIAL. EACH PLAYER NEEDS TO KNOW WHERE HE HAS TO BE, AND THAT IS WHY THERE NEEDS TO BE MUTUAL UNDERSTANDING BECAUSE YOU NEED ABSOLUTE DISCIPLINE.

LOUIS VAN GAAL

Diet and professionalism are essential if you want to keep playing for a long time. How you train and prepare is just as important as what you do on the pitch.

FRANCO BARESI

You can walk around thinking you're a winner, but if you don't train like a winner or if you don't do everything in your life to maintain being a winner, it just stops there.

VINCENT KOMPANY

As always with success in any walk of life, the key is working hard for the team. But I don't really see it as work. I see being a football manager as a way to live.

ROBERTO MARTÍNEZ

THE ESSENCE OF
FOOTBALL

IS THE ART OF
TEAMWORK.

THE MORE DIFFICULT THE VICTORY, THE GREATER THE HAPPINESS IN WINNING.

PELÉ

After the problems with my shoulders
I needed to bulk up and make myself
stronger... People probably don't realise
it, but you often have to train harder
when you're injured than when you're fit.

THEO WALCOTT

I don't think you can overcome
your opponents by tactics alone. You
also need passion and match-
winning individuals.

AIMÉ JACQUET

Maturity and experience taught
me that I have to surround myself
with my people, to feel good about
myself, and to forget about the bad
moments... Every night, I sleep well
and I get up with the same passion
that I've had since I was a kid.

SERGIO RAMOS

Knowing that mistakes do happen makes
it easier to deal with them, but the key
thing is that you learn from the mistake
and make an effort to improve.

HOWARD WEBB

That never-say-die mentality is
something I've had all my life. In school,
if it was football, cricket, basketball,
anything – I always wanted to be
the best I could be.

GARY PALLISTER

Football is the most important thing in the world. I don't know of anything else in the world you can get such an emotional jolt from, to go so quickly from anger to bliss in two minutes.

SAMUEL ETO'O

Wherever you are, whoever you are, you can achieve your dreams if you work hard. So don't give up, and keep trying because everything is possible.

MICHAEL ESSIEN

If you're interested in finding out more
about our books, find us on Facebook at
Summersdale Publishers and follow us
on Twitter at **@Summersdale**.

www.summersdale.com